Hope lies in dreams,
in imagination,
and in the courage of those
who dare to make dreams
into reality.
—Dr. Jonas Salk

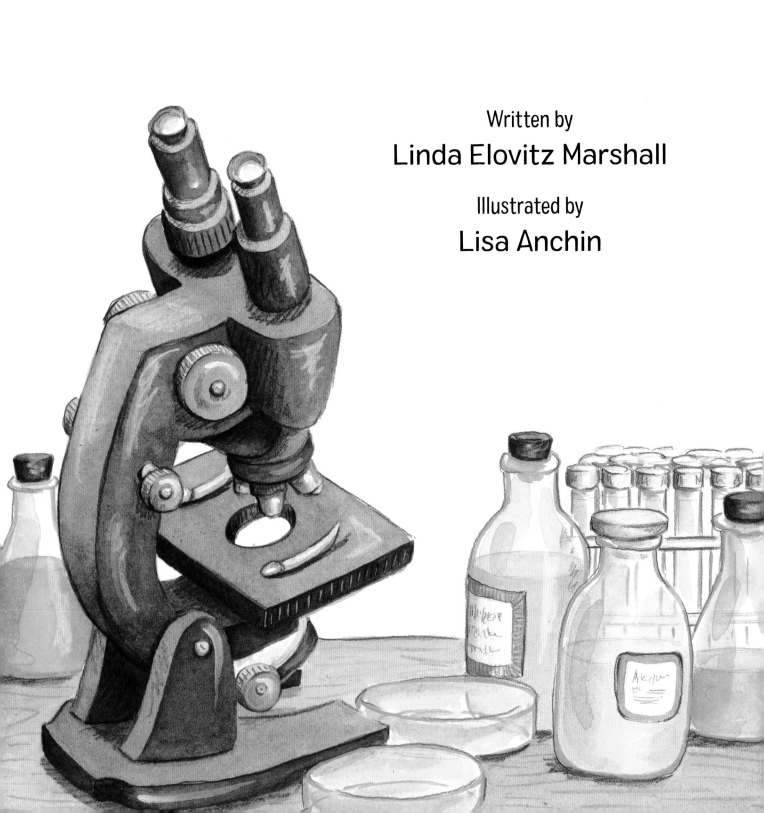

Written by

Linda Elovitz Marshall

Illustrated by

Lisa Anchin

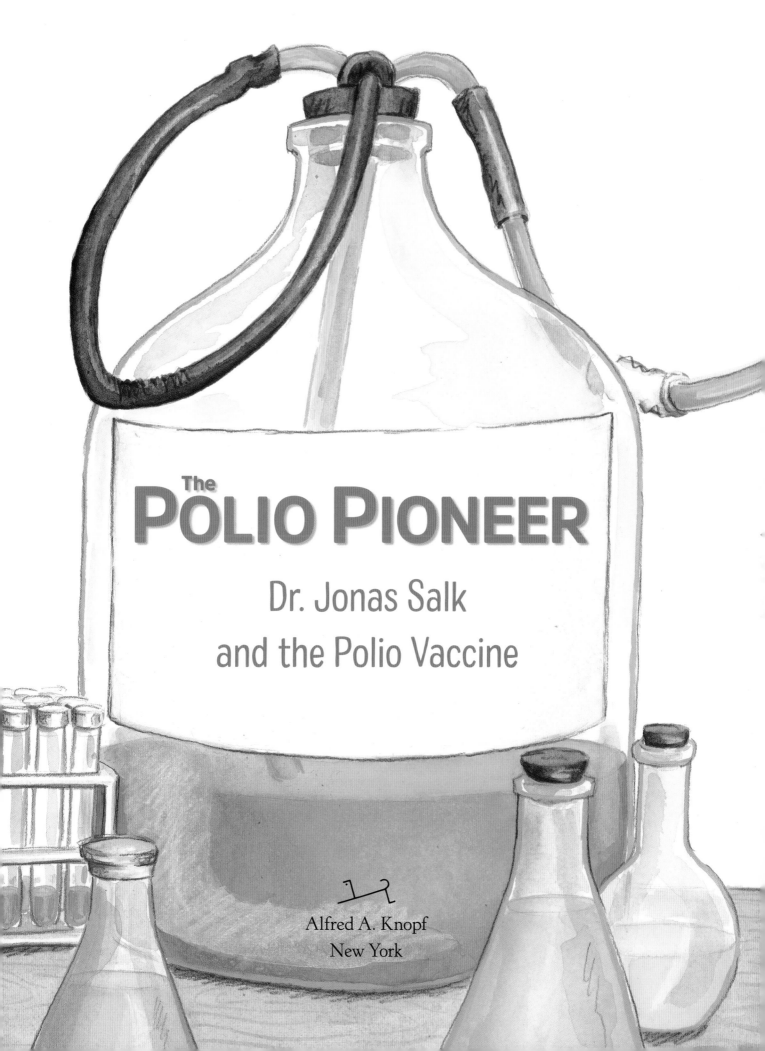

The POLIO PIONEER

Dr. Jonas Salk
and the Polio Vaccine

Alfred A. Knopf

New York

People at the victory parade in New York City cheered.
"Hip, hip, HOORAY!
Hip, hip, HOORAY!
The war's over!"
It was 1918. The First World War had ended.
But four-year-old Jonas Salk didn't cheer.
Jonas saw injured and wounded soldiers.
He saw soldiers unable to walk.

Jonas Salk was a kid who saw things differently.

While friends played games, Jonas read and read. . . .

But when they needed a referee, they asked Jonas for help.

He knew the rules and applied them fairly.

Jonas's family was Jewish. They fled Russia and Lithuania to escape religious persecution.

They came to America seeking safer, better lives.

His mother, Dora, had little formal education.

After coming to America, she learned to speak English.

But when Jonas was a child, she could read and write only in Yiddish.

His father, Daniel, was an excellent lacemaker, but he was often out of work . . . and there was never enough money.

Yet Dora and Daniel taught their children the importance of education, of kindness, and of doing good works.

Jonas prayed that he might, someday, help make the world a better place.

Jonas attended the City College of New York, where tuition was free and where, unlike at many other colleges and universities, Jews were welcome.

There, he discovered . . . CHEMISTRY!

Jonas hoped that by understanding science, he could make medicines that would help people.

He decided to go to medical school to become a doctor and researcher.

After medical school, Dr. Jonas Salk worked with his teacher and friend Dr. Thomas Francis.

They were seeking a medicine to protect people from influenza—the "flu" virus—which, in 1918, killed millions of people around the world.

Substances known as vaccines had already been made to help protect people against other diseases.

Dr. Salk and Dr. Francis had an idea.

What if a person was given some flu virus that was killed by chemicals so it could not cause disease?

Then could that person's body "practice" fighting the flu?
Could that person's body learn to fight the flu virus . . . and WIN?
Dr. Salk and Dr. Francis thought it could.

They studied different types of influenza viruses.

Then, using inactivated flu viruses, they made a vaccine to give people's bodies a safe "practice" run.

Dr. Francis and Dr. Salk's flu vaccine worked!
Their "flu shot" helped prevent people from getting the flu.
It helped give people *immunity* to the flu.
Since then, flu shots have saved thousands of lives each year.

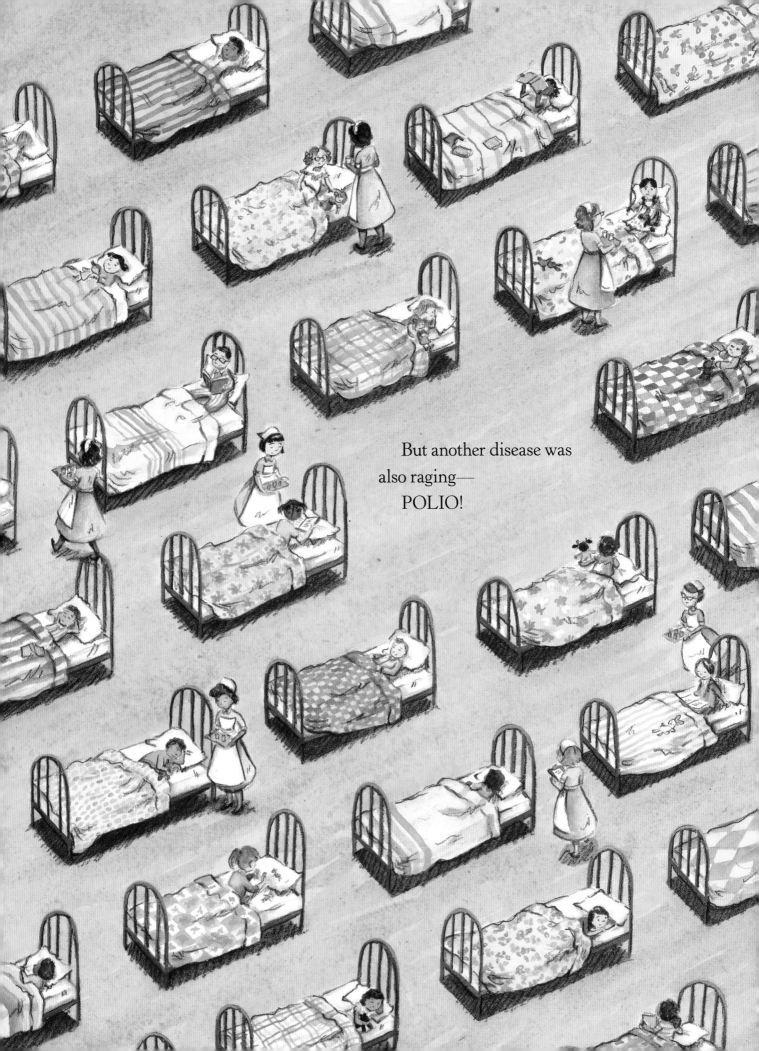

But another disease was
also raging—
POLIO!

Throughout America, polio paralyzed or killed thousands of
people every year, including many babies and small children.
No one could be sure they were safe from the disease.
Not even future US president Franklin Delano Roosevelt.

Fearing that polio could spread through water,
communities closed swimming pools and beaches.
Parents kept children away from movie theaters,
sleepovers, and crowds.

Everywhere, people wondered: Could polio be prevented? Could it be cured?

Dr. Salk believed polio could be prevented.
He believed he could develop a polio vaccine.
Dr. Salk researched, experimented, and tested ideas.

He and his team of scientists labored day
and night, night and day.

Dr. Salk and his team studied different types of polio viruses.

Just as with the flu vaccine, they killed the polio viruses with chemicals so the viruses couldn't cause disease.

Then they used the inactive polio viruses to make a vaccine.

Dr. Salk and his team first tested their vaccine in Pittsburgh, Pennsylvania, where they lived.

Dr. Salk gave many of the shots himself.

The vaccine appeared safe and seemed to strengthen the body's defense against polio, but . . . would it *actually* prevent polio?

A larger test—with many more participants—was needed.

Dr. Francis joined in to oversee the larger test.

Throughout America, almost two million children—

POLIO PIONEERS!—participated.

On April 12, 1955, Dr. Francis announced to the world:

"The vaccine WORKS!"

POLIO could be CONQUERED!

Church bells RANG! Factory whistles BLEW!
The country CELEBRATED!

Within a few years, cases of polio plummeted.

Soon, throughout America and much of the world,
polio was almost completely gone.

But more research and work on other diseases was needed.

Dr. Salk wanted to make sure all people around the world received vaccinations . . . and stayed healthy.

So Dr. Salk kept working, thinking, dreaming.

And on a bluff overlooking the Pacific Ocean, Dr. Salk established the Salk Institute for Biological Studies. There, researchers question and discover, seeking cures for cancer, HIV/AIDS, diabetes, multiple sclerosis, and many other diseases.

Jonas Salk was a kid who saw things
differently, a kid who wanted to help make
the world a better place. . . .
Ever meet a kid like that?
Could that kid be YOU?

AUTHOR'S NOTE

When I was a child in the 1950s, my friends and I couldn't go swimming in pools, lakes, or ponds. We couldn't go to movies, either. Why? Polio! Each summer, the disease raged. My mother, like parents throughout the country, did her best to protect me. She kept me from crowds and public swimming places. One summer, she even moved our family to a smaller city, where, she thought, polio was less likely to strike.

I was little, but I knew about polio. A boy in my neighborhood got the disease. He recovered. But not completely. After polio, he was never able to walk without a crutch.

Then came the polio vaccine . . . and freedom! Within a few years of its discovery, enough people were vaccinated and protected from the disease that my friends and I could go to pools, lakes, and ponds. We could go to the movies, too.

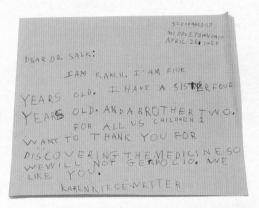

Dr. Salk became my hero. He changed the lives of children all over the world. Partly in tribute to Dr. Jonas Salk, my husband (a family physician) and I named our first son Jonah.

Thanks to Dr. Salk and the teams of scientists he worked with, we have vaccines that help protect us against polio and influenza. Other scientists, beginning with Dr. Edward Jenner and his work on smallpox prevention in 1796, also developed vaccines. These days, vaccines prevent diphtheria, pertussis/whooping cough, tetanus, measles, mumps, rubella, and many other diseases. All have helped make us safer and helped make our world a better place.

I wanted to share Dr. Salk's story with generations that, thankfully, no longer need to fear polio. I was lucky enough to receive a grant that enabled me to visit and tour the Salk Institute for Biological Studies in La Jolla, California. The Institute's librarian introduced

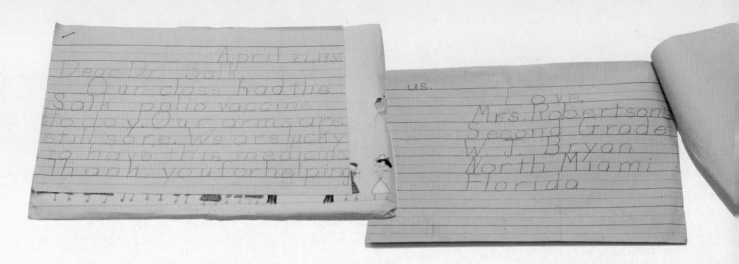

April 21, 1955

Dear Dr. Salk,
Our class had the Salk polio vaccine today. Our arms are still sore. We are lucky to have this medicine. Thank you for helping

us.

Love,
Mrs. Robertson's Second Grade
W. J. Bryan
North Miami
Florida

me to source materials, including *Jonas Salk: A Life* by Charlotte DeCroes Jacobs. I also learned more from Dr. Salk's children, Dr. Peter Salk, Dr. Darrell Salk, and Dr. Jonathan Salk. The photos on these pages of the children's letters were taken by Michael Salk, grandson of Dr. Jonas Salk. The Salk family has been very gracious in helping me with this project. I truly appreciate their interest and assistance.

Jonas Salk was a kid who cared about other people and who wasn't afraid of hard work. He grew up to become what, in Yiddish, is called a mensch. May Dr. Salk's good works, kindness, and dedication inspire others to help make the world a better place.

Thank you, Dr. Salk!

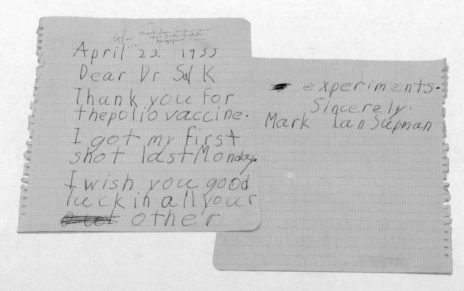

April 23, 1955
Dear Dr. Salk
Thank you for the polio vaccine.
I got my first shot last Monday.
I wish you good luck in all your other
experiments.
Sincerely,
Mark Ian Siepman

Many children sent thank-you letters to Dr. Salk. These photos—taken by Michael Salk, Dr. Salk's grandson—show just a few of the letters he received. They are part of the Jonas Salk Papers in the University of California-San Diego Library's Special Collections and Archives and are provided courtesy of the library and of Michael Salk.

SOURCES

Books

Bankston, John. *Jonas Salk and the Polio Vaccine*. Newark, DE: Mitchell Lane Publishers, 2001.

Curson, Marjorie. *Jonas Salk*. Morristown, NJ: Silver Burdett Press, 1990.

Jacobs, Charlotte DeCroes. *Jonas Salk: A Life*. New York: Oxford University Press, 2015.

Kluger, Jeffrey. *Splendid Solution: Jonas Salk and the Conquest of Polio*. New York: G. P. Putnam's Sons, 2004.

Krohn, Katherine, and Al Milgrom (illustrator). *Jonas Salk and the Polio Vaccine*. Mankato, MN: Capstone, 2006.

McPherson, Stephanie Sammartino. *Jonas Salk: Conquering Polio*. Minneapolis: Lerner, 2001.

Oshinsky, David M. *Polio: An American Story*. New York: Oxford University Press, 2006.

Sherrow, Victoria. *Jonas Salk: Beyond the Microscope*. New York: Chelsea House, 2008.

Interviews and Other Media

"Jonas Salk, M.D. Biography—Academy of Achievement." Academy of Achievement. December 14, 2016. Web. July 2017. achievement.org/achiever/jonas-salk-m-d/#interview

Peter Salk, M.D. Telephone interview conducted by Linda Elovitz Marshall (author). November 21, 2016.

THIS IS A BORZOI BOOK PUBLISHED BY ALFRED A. KNOPF

Text copyright © 2020 by Linda Elovitz Marshall
Jacket art and interior illustrations copyright © 2020 by Lisa Anchin

All rights reserved. Published in the United States by Alfred A. Knopf, an imprint of Random House Children's Books, a division of Penguin Random House LLC, New York.

Knopf, Borzoi Books, and the colophon are registered trademarks of Penguin Random House LLC.

Visit us on the Web! rhcbooks.com
Educators and librarians, for a variety of teaching tools, visit us at RHTeachersLibrarians.com

Library of Congress Cataloging-in-Publication Data is available upon request.
ISBN 978-0-525-64651-8 (hc) — ISBN 978-0-525-64652-5 (lib. bdg.)
ISBN 978-0-525-64653-2 (ebook)

The text of this book is set in 14-point Horley Old Style.
The illustrations were created using acrylic gouache and pencil.

Book design by Nicole de las Heras

MANUFACTURED IN CHINA
August 2020
10 9 8 7 6 5 4 3 2 1
First Edition

To my beloved Bob, with thanks for your untiring help;
to Dena, Jonah, Benjamin, Rebecca;
and to Gabriel, Niomi, Julia Rose, Avigail,
Lyra, Talia, Leah, Noa, Baruch,
Ezra, Aviya, Orly, and Ellie.
—L.E.M.

For Elizabeth
and all those who dedicate their lives
to the pursuit of knowledge
—L.A.